796.357 Bliss, Jonathan.
BLI   Home run leaders

Marion Center Area School
Creekside-Washington Library

HOME RUN LEADERS

Jonathan Bliss

The Rourke Corporation, Inc.
Vero Beach, Florida 32964

Copyright 1991 by The Rourke Corporation, Inc.

All rights reserved. No part of this book may be reproduced or utilized in any form or by any means, electronic or mechanical, including photocopying, recording or by any information storage and retrieval system without permission in writing from the publisher.

The Rourke Corporation, Inc.
P.O. Box 3328, Vero Beach, FL 32964

Bliss, Jonathan.
    Home run leaders / by Jonathan Bliss.
       p. cm — (Baseball heroes)
    Includes bibliographical references and index.
    Summary: Looks at the historic achievements of baseball's heavy hitters, the home run sluggers, including the likes of Rogers Hornsby, Hank Greenberg, Mickey Mantle, and of course Babe Ruth and Hank Aaron.
    ISBN 0-86593-128-3
       1. Baseball players—United States—Biography—Juvenile literature. 2. Home runs (Baseball)—Juvenile literature. [1. Baseball players. 2. Home runs (Baseball)] I. Title. II. Series.
GV865.A1B584   1991
796.357'092'2—dc20   91-9740
[B]   CIP
                                                                                                             AC

Series Editor: Gregory Lee
Editor: Marguerite Aronowitz
Book design and production: The Creative Spark, Capistrano Beach, CA
Cover photograph: Darrell Sandler/SportsLight
Consultant: Chris Rourke

Contents

A Homer By Any Other Name	5
Golden Bats	11
Post-War Bombers	21
The Era Of Aaron	29
Modern Mashers	35
Glossary	44
Bibliography	45
Index	46

Cecil Fielder became the first major leaguer to break the 50-plus home run mark in a single season since 1977.

A Homer By Any Other Name

On the last day of the 1990 season, Cecil Fielder stepped to the plate in Tiger Stadium. For weeks he'd been trying to do something no player had done in 13 years: hit 50 home runs in one season. But the home runs weren't coming for Cecil. He'd been stuck on 49 homers for two weeks—trying too hard to hit the long ball, and striking out too much. Now, on the last day, most of the sportswriters and fans present in the stadium didn't expect him to make it.

When Fielder had his first at-bat, he swung poorly and grounded out. The next time, he seemed to be calmer, waiting longer for a look at the ball. When it

Home Run Trivia

Q: Who has hit the most home runs in a single season?
A: Roger Maris hit 61 in 1961.

Q: Who has the most career home runs?
A: Henry "Hammerin' Hank" Aaron.

Q: What great Negro League player hit 75 homers in a season?
A: Josh Gibson.

Q: What team did Hank Aaron play for when he hit his 715th homer?
A: Atlanta Braves.

Q: Name the players tied for 12th on the all-time home run list.
A: Eddie Mathews and Ernie Banks.

Q: Who was the last player to hit more than 50 homers in a season?
A: Cecil Fielder.

Cubs' shortstop sensation Ryne Sandberg hit the most home runs (40) in the National League in 1990.

arrived, he was ready, hitting it solid and sending it into the second tier beyond the left field wall. Homer number 50. For good measure, he hit number 51 the next time up, becoming only the eleventh player in major league history to hit 50 or more homers in a season!

Round-tripper, long ball, dinger, tater, four-bagger: call it what you will, the home run (or HR) is one of the most exciting moments in baseball. Of all the hits a batter can get, the homer is the rarest. It requires not only perfect timing, but strength to launch the ball off the bat and send it over the outfield fence. In many modern ballparks this is difficult to do. In others—like Royal Stadium in Kansas City or the Houston Astrodome—it is almost impossible.

Players who hit a lot of home runs have always been highly prized, even though they don't always have the highest batting average on their team. They may strike out a lot, but if they can deliver the big hit when it really counts, they become the fans' hero. Throughout baseball history there have been hundreds of batters who have hit over .300 in a season, but there are less than a dozen players who've hit more than 50 home runs in one year. Only five have ever hit over 50 homers in one year more than once in their career, and only two players have ever hit 60 or more home runs in a single season.

In The Beginning

When people first started playing baseball, it was a sport of fast feet and loose wrists. A player usually tried to put the ball in play and trust to his speed to advance him. Driving the ball as far as he could wasn't the most important part of the game.

One of the reasons for this was the baseball itself. Modern baseballs have a cork center and are wound tightly with fine wool thread. They bounce. But baseballs of the 1800s were called "dead balls." They had a soft rubber center, loosely wound with string. They were larger and heavier than today's baseball—more like a well-used softball. It took really solid contact to launch one over the outfield fence. In 1876, a Philadelphia player named G. Hall led the National League (NL) with only five home runs! The following year, Paul Hines blasted just four home runs to lead the league.

As the new century began, the most famous home run hitter was John Franklin "Home Run" Baker who earned his nickname by leading the league in home runs

Unusual for a leadoff hitter like Rickey Henderson is his home run stats: he was sixth in the AL in 1990 with 28.

four times: nine in 1911, ten in 1912, 12 in 1913, and eight in 1914. Baker displayed good timing in the 1914 World Series when he collected two of his home runs and led the Philadelphia A's to the championship.

There were many ballplayers in the dead ball era who might have hit more homers had it not been for the sheer difficulty of it. In 1913, the entire American League (AL) managed only 160 homers (only two more than the Baltimore Orioles hit all by themselves in 1983). In 1915 Bob Roth hit only seven homers for Cleveland, but it was enough to lead the American League.

Veteran Carlton Fisk has hit more home runs than any other catcher in major league history—more than 327.

Golden Bats

The National League started using the cork-center or "live ball" in 1911. By 1915, this smaller and livelier baseball was putting a new kick in the game of baseball.

With the new ball there was a 45-point increase in batting averages between 1915 and 1925. But the increase in averages was nothing compared to the increase in home runs: from 384 in 1915 to 1,565 in 1930.

The home run was suddenly big business, and a whole new generation of heroes intent on destroying old home run records was born.

Rogers Hornsby

Rogers Hornsby is ranked by many as the greatest right-handed hitter of all time. He played in his first major league game in 1915. Hornsby played infield for the Cardinals, usually at second base, from 1916 through 1926. From 1920 through 1925 he won six consecutive batting titles (an NL record). In those six years he batted over .400 three times, setting the modern season record for highest average: .424. During the same period he led the NL in home runs (twice), RBIs (three times), and base hits (four times). Before Hornsby's 42-homer season, no National Leaguer had ever hit more than 24 homers in a season! Over his entire career, Hornsby compiled a remarkable .358 batting average, second only to Ty Cobb.

The Babe—George Herman Ruth—had the record for most career home runs (714) for over 40 years before Hank Aaron broke it in 1974.

Babe Ruth

Of all the men who ever picked up a bat, no one matched George Herman "Babe" Ruth. But he first gained fame as a pitcher. During the six seasons Ruth pitched with the Boston Red Sox, his record was 89-46. He set a record for scoreless innings pitched in World Series play.

Ruth was probably the best pitcher in the major leagues at the time, and he became an even better hitter. Burly and barrel-chested, Ruth swung gracefully. He rounded the bases on spindly legs that could move surprisingly fast for a big man. Eventually his incredible batting talent persuaded his manager to put him in the outfield. In 1919, the six-foot, two-inch left-hander set a major league record with 29 home runs, even though the dead ball was still in use.

Playing with the New York Yankees from 1919 to 1935, Ruth ruled the major leagues. He put up incredible numbers every year. In 1919, while still pitching for Boston, the Babe socked 29 homers—twice as many as any other American League player since the beginning of the century. The following year, Ruth hit 54 homers for New York. In 1921, he hit 59.

During the course of his career, Ruth led the league in home runs 12 times. Three times he hit more than 50: 1920 (54); 1922 (59); and his greatest year, 1927, when he hit 60. His record was so incredible that most sportswriters at that time doubted whether anyone would ever equal it. In fact, no one did until Roger Maris hit number 61 in 1961. But it took him an additional ten games to do it. No one has reached that number since.

Ruth not only hit homers in the regular season, he also held the record for most homers in the World Series and All-Star games. Baseball lore is full of stories about

Ruth's home runs. Perhaps the greatest is the one told about how the Babe pointed to the bleachers during the 1932 World Series. On the next pitch, he hit the ball right to that spot for a game-winning home run.

Ruth never lost his ability to hit the long ball, even though he grew older and heavier. In his last game in 1935, Ruth hit three homers. This brought his career total to 714, a record that lasted until Henry Aaron beat it half a century later.

In 1936 he was elected as a charter member of baseball's Hall of Fame, along with Ty Cobb, Honus Wagner, and Tris Speaker. Even today, Babe Ruth is recognized as the finest all-around player ever to play the game.

Hack Wilson

While Babe Ruth was crushing homers in the American League, Hack Wilson was doing a good job in the National League. His baseball career didn't begin until he was 21 years old. Hugely muscular, Wilson was soon hitting home runs in bunches. He joined the Chicago Cubs in 1926 and paced the National League in home runs from 1926 to 1928.

1930 was Wilson's finest year. He hit 56 home runs and drove home 190 runs—both National League records that have never been equaled. During a 12-year major league career Wilson led the NL in home runs four times and compiled 1,461 hits, including 244 homers and 1,062 RBIs.

Jimmie Foxx

Jimmie Foxx was discovered playing high school baseball by Frank "Home Run" Baker, one of the great home run hitters of the 19th century. Baker knew what

Jimmie Foxx had a fence-busting season in 1932 when he punched 58 homers: two shy of Babe Ruth's record of 60.

he was seeing in Foxx, and changed him from an infielder to a catcher. By 1928 Foxx was starting regularly for the Philadelphia A's, and his first full year he batted .328.

For seven more seasons and three World Series (1929-1931) Foxx starred for the Athletics, averaging 41 homers per season with his unique straddle stance. His 58 round-trippers in 1932 fell only two short of Babe Ruth's record 60. During that season he also hit .364, got 169 RBIs, and slugged 100 extra-base hits.

Jimmie Foxx was traded to the Boston Red Sox in 1935, where he continued to hit homers in Fenway Park. In 1938 he hit 50 homers—one of only five players to hit 50 or more homers in one season twice in his career.

Foxx swatted some of the longest home runs ever hit in AL ballparks. He collected 534 career homers and drove in 1,922 runs (sixth best lifetime). And he won three home run championships in an era when he was competing against the likes of Lou Gehrig and Babe Ruth for the honor.

Lou Gehrig

Imagine being a pitcher and facing both Babe Ruth and Lou Gehrig on the same New York Yankees team. Gehrig joined the Yankees in 1925, and never left the lineup. Many baseball historians believe that the 1927 Yankees, anchored by Ruth and Gehrig, was the greatest baseball team of all time.

The left-handed Gehrig beat Ruth in many categories. He batted .373 and led the AL in doubles and total bases. Gehrig scored and knocked in over 100 runs for 13 straight seasons. In 1931 he slugged 46 home runs, becoming baseball's top run producer by scoring 163 with a record 184 RBIs. He won the Triple Crown of hitting (leading the league in home runs, batting, and RBIs) three times: 1927, 1934, and 1937.

On June 3, 1932, he became the first AL player ever to hit four home runs in one game. Gehrig also compiled a career record 23 grand slam homers. Sadly, at the age of 35, the Iron Horse developed a rare muscle disease (afterwards known as Lou Gehrig's Disease) which forced his early retirement and claimed his life a few years later.

Hank Greenberg

Hank Greenberg was a star with the Detroit Tigers from 1933 until 1946. From the beginning, Greenberg hit the long ball easily. He had a big, roundhouse swing, and rarely hit line drives. Most of his homers were towering shots that would carry into the upper decks of any stadium.

Because of the four-and-one-half seasons Hank lost to military service during World War II, Greenberg's career 331 home runs and 1,276 RBIs do not fully reflect his greatness as a home run hitter. Over his shortened career he won the American League home run title four times (1935, 1938, 1940, and 1946). No right-handed batter has surpassed his 1938 total of 58 home runs in one season.

Only four players have ever exceeded Greenberg's career slugging percentage of .605. He was elected to the Hall of Fame in 1956.

Ralph Kiner

Following World War II, Ralph Kiner went directly from a soldier's uniform to a Pittsburgh Pirates' uniform. He didn't waste his opportunity. In 1946 Kiner started a home run record that neither Babe Ruth nor any other slugger has ever equaled. For seven consecutive years he either led or shared the National League lead in home runs.

Kiner enjoyed two of the most productive home run years a National Leaguer ever had. In 1947 he slugged 51 round trippers and set a major league record by hitting eight homers over four games. In two games that year, he hit three home runs in a row. Then, in 1949, Ralph slammed 54 homers.

Kiner never missed a game. One day, a fever of

101 degrees prevented him from being in the lineup. But when he heard that the opponents had gone ahead 10-8, he suited up and reported to the dugout. After telling his coach "I have one good swing in me," Kiner produced a game-winning grand slam homer!

Josh Gibson

One of the greatest home run hitters of all time never had a chance to play in the major leagues because he was black. His name was Joshua "Josh" Gibson, and many people still consider him to be the finest catcher ever to play the game.

The son of a sharecropper and millworker, Josh grew up in an era when major league baseball was still a white man's game. Black men were limited to playing in what was called the Negro League. Many great players who happened to be black never saw action in the major leagues because of racism.

In 1927, when Josh was 15, he joined the semi-pro Pittsburgh Crawfords. Three years later, the powerfully built six-foot, two-inch Gibson joined the Homestead Grays of the American Negro League. His home runs at Yankee Stadium and Forbes Field in Pittsburgh were the longest ever hit in both parks. In 1931, the 19-year-old Gibson hit 75 home runs and quickly became a star.

From 1937 to 1946, Gibson and teammate Buck Leonard were considered the Negro League's Babe Ruth and Lou Gehrig. Together they helped the Grays win nine consecutive championships. In fact, Gibson never played for a losing team. Due to poor record keeping, his home run hitting totals cannot be fully documented. However, reliable estimates place his total homers in the Negro Leagues at 960!

How good was Josh Gibson? In exhibition matches

Hall of Famer Josh Gibson never played in the major leagues. Because of racism, he played in the American Negro League. But his 900-plus career home runs make him one of the greatest hitters in baseball history.

against major league players, he batted well against the major league's great pitchers: Grover Cleveland Alexander, Dizzy Dean, and Bob Feller. Joe DiMaggio emulated Gibson's stance, and many other players considered Josh Gibson to be the greatest home run hitter they ever saw. In 1972, Gibson was elected to the Hall of Fame.

Two-time MVP Dale Murphy has over 370 lifetime home runs.

Post-War Bombers

The Great Depression and World War II took their toll on baseball. Attendance declined during the 1930s and '40s, then the war took most of the great ballplayers of the era— including Joe DiMaggio and Ted Williams—off to the battlefield. After they returned, the game gained in popularity again. The '50s and '60s were a time for renewed interest in baseball, and with the larger attendance came bigger-than-life heroes.

Ted Williams

If there was ever a player who was born to hit, it was Ted Williams. From the very start he had a power swing. In his first season Ted hit .327 and was named AL Rookie of the Year. In 1941, Ted hit .402, the youngest player ever to break the .400 barrier.

Williams could do anything he wanted to on the baseball diamond. When he retired in 1960 after 19 years in Boston, Williams had achieved career marks that still stand out: second ever in walks (2,019), slugging percentage (.634), and sixth all-time in batting average (.344). Williams was named to every All-Star Game from 1940 to 1960.

Many fine hitters don't have home run power, but Williams showed tremendous power to all fields. He led the AL four times in homers. His secret to hitting long

The durable Harmon Killebrew hit 573 home runs in his Hall of Fame career.

balls was no secret at all: he simply hit the ball hard every time he was at the plate. Williams' career home run total of 521 places him tenth on the all-time list.

Mickey Mantle

Mickey Mantle was the biggest Yankee star of the 1950s and '60s. His rookie season was nothing special, but later Mantle became a Yankee superstar, leading the club in home runs and batting almost every season. By the time he retired in 1968, the Mick had slugged 536 homers (eighth on the all-time list).

Four times during his career Mantle won the AL home run championship: 1955, 1956, 1958, and 1960. He is one of only five players to hit 50 homers in two seasons: 52 in 1956 and 54 in 1961. The Mick is still credited with one of the longest home runs of all time: a shot he hit in Yankee Stadium that traveled more than 700 feet before hitting a wall.

Roger Maris

Roger Maris and the number 61 will always be remembered together. That's because no major leaguer has ever hit 61 homers in just one season. No one, that is, except Roger Maris.

In 1959, Maris was traded to the Yankees, where the right-hander reached his potential as a long-ball hitter and left an unforgettable mark on baseball history. In 1961 Maris and his teammate, Mickey Mantle, dueled for the home run title. After hitting only one homer in April, Maris belted 11 in May, 15 in June, 13 more in July, 11 in August, and nine in September. His record-breaking 61st home run came on October 1, the last day of the regular season, when he slammed a pitch off Tracy Stallard into the bleachers, passing Babe Ruth's 1927 mark of 60 in one season.

That same year, Maris belted seven homers in six straight games and tied an AL record for most homers in a doubleheader (4). He won the AL MVP award as well as the Hickok Trophy for the world's top pro athlete of 1961.

Harmon Killebrew

Harmon Killebrew was known in his playing days as "The Killer." Just by looking at him, you could tell why. At six feet and 195 pounds, the right-handed Killebrew resembled a wrestler more than a baseball player. In his days as a minor-league player, he had a

Roger Maris dueled with fellow Yankee slugger Mickey Mantle for the most home runs in a season. Maris still has the record: 61.

.847 batting average!

In 1959 Killebrew finally made it to the big leagues for good and immediately attracted attention by belting eight home runs in 12 days. By midseason, he'd slugged 28 homers and was chosen for the All-Star team. He finished the year with 42 homers to tie for the 1960 AL title.

Killebrew led the AL five times in homers and three times in RBIs. His home run total exceeded 40 in eight seasons, and he hit two round-trippers in one game 46 times. The Killer hit four on one memorable day in 1963! Killebrew's average of one HR every 14.2 at bats is third on the all-time list behind Babe Ruth and Ralph Kiner, and his home run total of 573 ranks fifth all-time.

Willie Mays

Willie Mays always had a smile for everyone, even the pitchers he routinely bombed from home plate. Mays was only 19 when he was signed by the New York Giants, where he became their regular center fielder. He helped the Giants win the NL pennant and was named Rookie of the Year.

With the Giants, who eventually moved to San Francisco, Mays amazed the crowds, batting over .300 ten times. He led the NL in home runs four times, slugging 51 in 1955 and 52 in 1965. He also hit more than 30 home runs in 11 different seasons.

Along with only a few other players, Mays once slugged four home runs in one game and twice hit three in one game. He was also very fast, becoming one of only six players to hit 30 home runs and steal 30 bases in the same season.

Mays retired in 1973 after a spectacular 22-year

Andre Dawson routinely clubs over 25 homers each season.

career with 3,283 hits, 660 home runs, 1,903 RBIs, and a .302 batting average. His 660 home runs rank him third on the all-time list behind Henry Aaron and Babe Ruth.

Willie McCovey

What Gehrig was to Ruth, and Maris was to Mantle, Willie McCovey was to Willie Mays. In his first game in the big leagues he went four for four, including two triples. He went on to earn NL Rookie of the Year honors. He soon became a favorite of Giants fans, combining with teammate Willie Mays to create one of the greatest one-two hitting pairs in baseball history.

A dead pull hitter, the left-handed McCovey hit line drives to right field, constantly threatening to reach the fence in any stadium in the National League. For example, in 1970, McCovey homered in 12 ball parks. He slugged three consecutive home runs twice in his career and belted two home runs in the same inning twice. In 1977, he hit grand slam and solo homers in the same inning!

As a result of his 22-year career, McCovey tied Ted Williams for ninth place on the all-time home run list. In 1986, McCovey was elected to the Hall of Fame.

The legendary Hank Aaron holds the career record for home runs: 755.

The Era Of Aaron

Like Josh Gibson, Hank Aaron began his career in the American Negro League. Unlike Gibson, he came along after the 1945 appearance of Jackie Robinson. It became obvious that black athletes were an important source of talent. Aaron spent only one year in the Negro League before he was signed by the Milwaukee Braves in 1952.

Almost immediately, Aaron became a star. He led the NL four times in home runs (1957, 1963, 1966 and 1967), RBIs and slugging percentage. He slugged 30 home runs and scored 100 runs or more 15 times in his career. The secret of his home run success was not great strength but his quick wrists which could turn on a ball and send it screaming into the bleachers.

Because of Aaron's great physical shape, he was able to play longer than most baseball players of his generation. He played all but two of his 23 seasons with the Braves. Between the ages of 35 and 40, he hit at least 34 home runs each year. When he hit 40 HRs in his fortieth year, it became clear that Babe Ruth's record of 714 lifetime homers was about to be broken.

That moment came one April evening in 1974. As thousands watched in Atlanta's Fulton County Stadium, and many more watched on television, Aaron connected with a 1-and-0 fastball from the L.A. Dodgers' Al Downing. It went sailing over the left field wall into the

Braves' bullpen, and Aaron rounded the bases as the stadium went wild. When he reached home plate his team and his mother were waiting to congratulate him.

In 1982, Aaron was inducted into the Hall of Fame, receiving more votes than anyone else except Ty Cobb and Willie Mays.

Frank Robinson

Frank Robinson came from Oakland, California, and excelled at baseball early in life. Following high school graduation, Robinson signed with the Cincinnati Reds and played for their minor league teams before joining the club in 1956. In his rookie year Robinson led the National League in runs scored, and tied a major league record for most home runs by a rookie: 38. It was no surprise when Robinson won the NL Rookie of the Year award.

Frank Robinson was everything a baseball player should be. Strong, quick, and graceful, he could field and bat with the best of them. Robinson was traded to the Baltimore Orioles following the 1965 season, and the next year became one of just 11 players to win baseball's Triple Crown. In 1966 he was selected the AL's MVP, becoming the only player to achieve this honor in both leagues.

In 1970 he tied a major league record by slugging grand slam home runs in back-to-back at-bats. Robinson was always a champion hitter: in 26 World Series games, Robinson hit eight homers and collected 23 hits.

In 1975 Robinson became player-manager for the Cleveland Indians—the first ever black major league manager. In all, Robinson hit 586 homers, fourth on the all-time list, and compiled a .294 lifetime batting average. In 1982, Robinson was elected to the Hall of Fame.

The Phillies' Mike Schmidt is seventh on the all-time home run list with 548.

Mike Schmidt

Mike Schmidt became the greatest power hitter in Philadelphia Phillies' history during the 1970s and '80s. After a short but excellent minor league career (1971-72), Schmidt became the Phillies' regular third baseman. In the beginning of his career he was a better defensive player—spearing line drives at third like few other fielders in the league. He also showed occasional flashes of power, like hitting 18 home runs. But he also struck out 136 times and hit only .196.

The right-hander blossomed in 1974 and won three consecutive home run titles (36, 38, 38). Altogether he led the National League in homers for eight seasons (1974-76, 1980-81, 1983-84, 1986). He broke Ralph Kiner's record of seven homer crowns. Schmidt's 548

Reggie Jackson stroked three home runs in just one game of the 1977 World Series, earning the nickname "Mr. October."

career home runs ranks seventh on the all-time list.

In 1976 Schmidt smacked four home runs in one game. He was the first National Leaguer to accomplish this since Willie Mays in 1965. Schmidt's best year was 1980 when he hit 48 HRs, the most in major league history by a third baseman. Schmidt's defensive game earned him ten Gold Gloves, second only to Baltimore's Brooks Robinson.

Schmidt was named the NL Most Valuable Player in 1980, 1981 and 1986. He led the Phillies to the 1980 World Series title over Kansas City and captured the World Series MVP as well. In 1983 he again led the Phillies into the World Series, but this time it was a losing cause. Schmidt retired from baseball in 1989.

Reggie Jackson

Few players have been better hitters under pressure than Reggie Jackson. Reggie grew up in suburban Philadelphia, winning letters in four sports at his high school.

Jackson played well with several minor league teams before joining the Athletics in 1967. He followed the club to Oakland and helped the A's win three consecutive World Series (1972-1974). During 1969 Jackson looked likely to pass the Babe Ruth-Roger Maris mark for most home runs in a season. He hit more than 30 home runs in the first half of the year, but then tailed off at the end of the season and finished with 47. It was an Athletic record, but not enough to break the record of 61. He was named 1973 AL MVP, leading the league with 32 home runs and 117 RBIs. In 1975 Jackson tied for the AL home run title. But despite his prowess with the bat, the A's owner traded him to Baltimore.

Jackson stayed in Baltimore one year, then got himself traded to the New York Yankees. With the Yankees, Reggie blossomed. In five years with New York, he hit 144 home runs. His World Series performances earned him the nickname "Mr. October." In five World Series, Jackson hit for a .755 slugging average, surpassing all players ever to appear in the post season. Jackson belted 10 World Series home runs, fifth on the all-time list.

Perhaps Jackson will be remembered for his All-Star performance in the deciding game of the 1977 Series. He hit three straight home runs on three first pitches off Dodger hurlers Burt Hooton, Elias Sosa, and Charlie Hough. The Series went to the Yanks. Only Babe Ruth had hit three homers in a World Series game before.

By the time Reggie retired in 1989, he'd collected 563 homers, sixth on the all-time list.

Mark McGwire's batting power has helped bring the Oakland A's to three World Series.

Modern Mashers

Today there's a new crop of home run hitters. Athletes seem to grow bigger now, but the stadiums they hit in are often bigger too. It takes a powerful swing to launch a ball out of places as roomy as the Houston Astrodome or the Royal's Stadium. Despite bigger parks, however, the balls keep rocketing out and new legends keep being born.

Mark McGwire

Mark McGwire was a member of the 1984 U.S. Olympic baseball team and the Oakland A's first-round draft choice that same year. After two years in the minors, he arrived in the big leagues with a bang. First he shattered the Major League record for rookie home runs by hitting 49, then he was chosen AL Rookie of the Year. At six-foot, five-inches and possessing a strong right-handed stroke, Mark began the 1987 season so strong that by the All-Star break he had 33 HRs. McGwire's bat cooled in August and September, but he still led the AL that season in both home runs and slugging percentage. He batted .289 with 118 RBIs. In 1988 McGwire's numbers dipped slightly to .260 with 32 home runs and 99 RBIs. His contributions helped earn the A's the AL pennant. In the World Series that year, his Game 3 solo home run in the bottom of the ninth resulted in a 2-1 win against the Dodgers. It was his only hit, however, and the A's lost the series.

In 1989 McGwire hit 33 home runs, collected 95 RBIs, and helped lead the A's to the World Series championship. The one-two punch of Oakland's "Bash Brothers"—McGwire and Jose Canseco—made the 1989 A's one of the toughest teams in the last 20 years. And the A's had Dave Henderson, Rickey Henderson, and Dave Parker to boot!

During the 1990 season McGwire continued hitting long balls. Despite injuries that kept him out for more than a dozen games, Mark put together 39 homers (second in the AL) and 108 RBIs (4th overall). He continues to be a mainstay of the club and should be a powerful hitter for years to come.

Jose Canseco

Few players lived up to their advance notices as well as Jose Canseco. Born in Havana, Cuba, Canseco became a baseball giant in both size and ability. He is the first-ever member of the "40-40" club, with 40 stolen bases and a league-leading 42 home runs in 1988. He also led the league with 124 RBIs and won the MVP award in a landslide vote.

Canseco spent only a few years in the minors before Oakland brought him up to the big leagues in 1985. In his first full season in the majors (1986), he hit 33 home runs and earned Rookie of the Year. With great bat speed and power to all fields, he became the first Oakland player with back-to-back 100 RBI seasons. He and McGwire have joined Dave Kingman as the A's only players having three straight 30-home run seasons. Two years of intense weight training improved Canseco's power and made him one of the most powerful batters ever to play the game. His defense has improved along

Jose Canseco started his own 40-40 club: the first player in history to hit 40 homers and steal 40 bases in a single season.

with his power, and he is now regarded as one of the better right fielders in the league.

Canseco's three homers in the League Championship Series matched George Brett's AL record. His home run in Game 4 of the 1988 World Series traveled more than 400 feet before denting a TV camera in deep center field! In Game 1 of the World Series, Canseco hit his first major league grand slam in the second inning—only the 16th time this has been done in World Series play.

1989 saw Canseco spend much of the season out of the line-up after wrist surgery. He returned the last third of the season and proceeded to go on a home run binge. Over only 89 games, Canseco hit 17 homers and collected 57 RBIs. Many players need an entire season to equal that. In post-season play, Canseco helped the A's to a World Series championship over San Francisco.

In 1990 Canseco was again plagued by injury, this time with a bad back. He was out of the lineup for more than a month. Even so, when he played he played big. He collected 37 homers, 101 RBIs, and a .274 batting average. One can only wonder what he might have done if he'd been healthy the entire year.

Bo Jackson

Bo Jackson is a rare athlete—a superstar in more than one pro sport. An All-Star football and baseball player at Auburn University, Bo was the 1985 Heisman Trophy winner. But he was also a great baseball player at Auburn. Jackson was drafted by both the Los Angeles Raiders football team and the Kansas City Royals. Rather than choose between the two sports, he did something few athletes ever try: he chose both.

As a halfback for the Los Angeles Raiders, he

Frank Robinson, who became the first black manager in the majors, has 586 career homers.

became one of the most exciting running backs in the NFL, having the highest per-rush average of any player.

As left fielder for the Royals, Jackson improved steadily over his first four major league seasons. After a brief stay in the minors, Kansas City brought Jackson up to the big club in 1986. In his first full year, 1987, Bo hit 22 homers. In 1988 he improved to 25 homers. In 1989 he hit 32 homers. In 1990, Bo hit 28 homers and earned a respectable .272 average, even though he missed the last month of the season. He was hurt while making a circus catch in the outfield. It was unlucky, because Bo had just hit three straight homers in the game!

Jackson suffers from the same problem as another heavy-hitting Jackson—Reggie. He strikes out a lot. In Bo's case, that was 172 times in 1990, a league high. But with his power he hit the ball not just past the fence, but clear out of the stadium. Several times over his first four years Jackson has hit the ball 600 feet.

In the 1989 All-Star game, Bo won the MVP award for a 500-foot blast he hit into straightaway center field, then followed it up with a run-scoring hit.

Cecil Fielder

No one knew who Cecil Fielder was at the beginning of the 1990 season. In fact, few people outside of Japan had ever heard of him.

Brought up to the big leagues by the Toronto Blue Jays in 1985, he hit .311 in a brief trial before being sent down to the minors. He surfaced again in 1987, hitting .269 with 14 home runs in a part-time role.

After the 1988 season, Toronto sold Fielder to Japan's Hanshin Tigers. It looked like Fielder would finish his baseball career in Japan, playing with other

Darryl Strawberry is always a dangerous hitter when it comes to the long ball.

Kevin Mitchell earned MVP honors for his 47-homer season in 1989.

major league "has beens." But something different happened. Through hard work and discipline, Fielder improved his game in Japan and became a superstar with the Tigers. A classic "late-bloomer," he became the home run champion of Japan in 1989.

The Detroit Tigers were looking for a home run hitter. They paid Fielder a lot of money to return, but few people in the league thought it was a good idea.

The last laugh was on Toronto. Fielder found Tiger Stadium in Detroit much to his liking. Almost immediately he began to hit the ball out of the park with an easy swing that killed the ball. As the months went by, Fielder's home run total climbed until at the end of September it stood at 49. Then, on the last day of the season, Fielder hit two home runs, becoming only the eleventh player to hit 50 or more home runs in a single season.

Fielder led the league in home runs, RBIs (132), and runs scored (104) while earning a .277 average. Maybe more hitters should play a season in Japan.

Who will be the next great home run hitters? Will there ever be another home run king as great as the ones who played the game in seasons past? Yes. As long as there are games to play, there will always be players who combine great skill with a good deal of luck to bring back memories of sluggers like Ruth, Gibson, Maris, and Aaron.

Glossary

BATTING AVERAGE. A statistic figured by dividing the number of hits a batter gets by the number of times he's at bat.

DEAD BALL. In the early days of the game, the baseball was larger, heavier, and didn't carry as far.

GRAND SLAM. A home run with the bases loaded.

LIVE BALL. Today's baseball is lighter, with a cork center, that travels farther when hit.

RBIs. Runs batted in. The number of base runners the batter manages to score during his time at bat.

SLUGGING PERCENTAGE. A statistic figured by dividing the total number of bases a batter gets by the number of times he's at bat.

TRIPLE CROWN. When a player ends the season leading the league in home runs, batting average, and RBIs.

WOOD. The bat. Aluminum bats are not allowed in the major leagues.

Bibliography

Astor, Gerald. *The Baseball Hall of Fame 50th Anniversary Book*. New York: Prentice-Hall, 1985.

Laird, A.W. *Ranking Baseball's Elite*. McFarland Press, 1990.

Mercurio, John A. *Record Profiles of Baseball's Hall of Famers*. Perennial Press, 1990.

Okrent, Daniel and Steve Wulf. *Baseball Anecdotes*. New York: Oxford University Press, 1989.

Porter, David L. *Biographical Dictionary of American Sports, Baseball*. Greenwood Press, 1987.

Reichler, Joseph, ed. *The Baseball Encyclopedia, 8th ed*. New York: Macmillan, 1990.

Shatzki, Mike ed. *The Ballplayers*. New York: Arbor House, 1990.

Index

Aaron, Henry ("Hank"), 5, 14, 27, 29-30, 43
American Negro League, 18, 29

Baker, John Franklin ("Home Run"), 7-9
Banks, Ernie, 5
batting averages, 11
Brett, George, 38

Canseco, Jose, 36-38
Cobb, Ty, 11, 14, 30

DiMaggio, Joe, 19, 21
dead ball, dead ball era, 7, 9

Fielder, Cecil, 5, 40-43
Foxx, Jimmie, 14-16

Gehrig, Lou, 16, 18, 27
Gibson, Josh, 5, 18-19, 29, 43
Greenberg, Hank, 17

Hall, G., 7
Hall of Fame (members), 14, 17, 19, 27, 30
Hines, Paul, 7
home runs (HRs), homers
   in World Series, 13, 33, 35, 38
   most (career), 14, 29-30
   most (season), 13, 15, 23, 33
Hornsby, Rogers, 11

Jackson, Bo, 38-40
Jackson, Reggie, 33, 40

Killebrew, Harmon, 23-25
Kiner, Ralph, 17-18, 25, 31
Kingman, Dave, 36

live ball, 11

Mantle, Mickey, 22-23, 27
Mathews, Eddie, 5

Maris, Roger, 5, 13, 23, 27, 33, 43
Mays, Willie, 25-27, 30, 32
McCovey, Willie, 27
McGwire, Mark, 35-36

Robinson, Frank, 30
Ruth, Babe, 13, 15, 16, 17, 18, 23, 25, 27, 29, 33, 43

Schmidt, Mike, 31-32
Speaker, Tris, 14

Triple Crown, 16, 30

Wagner, Honus, 14
Williams, Ted, 21-22, 27
Wilson, Hack, 14
World Series, 13, 15, 30, 32, 33, 35-36, 38

About The Author

Jonathan Bliss is the author of seven books, and he has written hundreds of computer and technology manuals. He holds degrees from Yale University, Edinburgh University in Scotland, and the University of Utah. He played baseball in high school and has been an unrepentant Red Sox fan his entire life.

Photo Credits

ALLSPORT USA: 4 (Brian Masck); 6, 10, 26 (Jonathan Daniel); 8 (Robert Beck); 20 (Lonnie Major); 28 (ALLSPORT); 31, 34 (Otto Greule, Jr.); 32 (V.J. Lovero); 39 (B. Schwartzman); 41 (Scott Halleran); 42 (John Swart)
National Baseball Library, Cooperstown, NY: 12, 15, 19, 24
Darrell Sandler/SportsLight: 37
UPI: 22